Bonnie
415 - 383 - 7122

A DESERT KINGDOM

The Rajputs of Bikaner

by Naveen Patnaik

Weidenfeld and Nicolson
London

First published in Great Britain in 1990
by George Weidenfeld & Nicolson Ltd
91 Clapham High Street, London SW4 7TA

Printed and bound in Italy by
Arti Grafiche Motta
Color separations by Colourscan, Singapore

A DESERT KINGDOM

TABLE OF CONTENTS

——— 9 ———

INTRODUCTION

——— 45 ———

LIFE IN BIKANER

——— 57 ———

PALACES, OLD AND NEW

——— 67 ———

SHIKAR THE SPORT OF MAHARAJAS

——— 79 ———

FESTIVALS AND WORSHIP

——— 85 ———

VICE REGAL VISITS

——— 95 ———

ROYAL ALLIANCES

——— 107 ———

A RAJPUT AT WAR

——— 113 ———

THE GOLDEN JUBILEE

INTRODUCTION

In the 15th century the ruler of Marwar, a kingdom on the western border of India so desolate it was known as the Land of Death, had fourteen sons all ambitious for territories of their own. One day, while holding court, the ruler observed his second son, Bika, deep in whispered conversation. Before the assembled princes and nobles, the king asked the young Bika if he was plotting the creation of his own kingdom. Bika took his father's jest as a challenge and left the kingdom, accompanied only by a small force of horsemen and soldiers. Turning north, he rode towards the great desert of India – the Thar.

On the borders of the desert was a region called Jangal Pradesh, or the Area of Wilderness, where Bika hoped to found his kingdom. Fired by dreams of conquest, his resolve was further strengthened by an encounter with a woman named Karniji, who was reputed to work miracles. When Bika asked for her blessings, Karniji placed her hand on the prince's head saying, "A brilliant future awaits you. In these lands your name and glory will be greater than your father's."

For the next thirty years Bika fought until he had succeeded in establishing a kingdom of his

own, The size of England, Bikaner was a sandy plateau with no rivers, peopled by desert nomads and peasants tilling parched fields. For the greater part of the year, coarse grass and camel-thorn was the only vegetation that could survive in the fierce heat, and even during the monsoon, the rainfall was scanty. But still the bards who had accompanied Bika on his quest for a kingdom sang:

Out of the silken darkness of a desert dawn,
Emerged the dream of Bikaner.

The kingdom of Bikaner may have been founded only five hundred years ago, but the history of its royal family dates from A.D. 470, when Nayn Pal conquered the wealthy state of Kanauj and established the Rathore dynasty. The victorious Rathores claimed descent from the sun itself and for eight centuries their dynasty prospered, until Muslim invaders sweeping through the passes of the mountains known as the Hindu Kush – the Tears of the Hindus – laid waste to the fertile kingdoms of Hindustan. In 1212 the rulers of Kanauj abandoned their ancestral home and marched towards the deserts of Rajputana in search of new domains, eventually

महाराजा- डूंगरसिंह जी

महाराजा- सरदारसिंह जी

महाराजा- अनूपसिंह जी

राजा- कर्णसिंह जी

Four rulers of Bikaner (clockwise):
Raja Karan Singh of Bikaner
(reigned 1631-1669) to whom the
Moghul Emperor Aurangzeb
granted a flourishing estate in
Southern India, whose villages still
bear the names of this monarch and
his sons. The versatile Maharaja
Anup Singh (reigned 1669-1698)
under whose genial patronage
Bikaner achieved her renaissance.
Maharaja Sardar Singh (reigned
1851-1872), who had eighteen

wives, ninety-nine elephants, and an
unnecessarily large military
establishment. He usually appeared
in splendid jewels, and his
extravagance coupled with support
of the British Raj virtually
bankrupted his state. Maharaja
Dungar Singh (reigned 1872-1887),
who ascended the throne at the age
of fifteen. During his rule, Bikaner
began its transition from a feudal
kingdom to a progressive state.

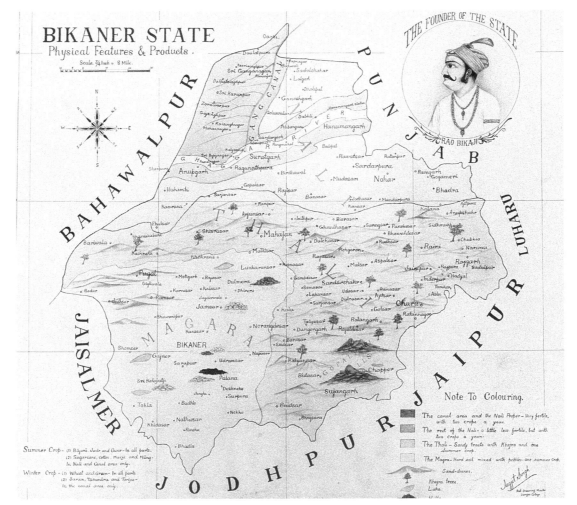

BIKANER STATE

Physical Features & Products.

Scale: 3/4 Inch = 8 Mile.

THE FOUNDER OF THE STATE

RAO BIKAJI

Note To Colouring.

The canal area and the Nali Proper - Very fertile, with two crops a year.

The rest of the Nali - a little less fertile, but with two crops a year.

The Thali - Sandy tracts with Khejra and one summer crop.

The Magra - Hard soil mixed with pebbles - one summer crop.

Sand-dunes.

Khejra trees.

Lake.

Hill.

Summer Crop - (1) Bajera, Jwar and Gwar - In all parts.
(2) Sugarcane, Cotton, Maize and Mung - In Nali and Canal areas only.

Winter Crop - (1) Wheat and Gram - In all parts.
(2) Sarson, Tahmuhna and Toriya - In the canal area only.

Jagjit Singh

Above right. A painting of Maharaja Sardar Singh, with a British officer, about to depart at the head of his troops to support the beleagured British during the Great Uprising of 1857.

Above left. Maharaja Rao Bika receiving the homage of his clansmen as well as that of the powerful chiefs he had subdued in 1488

Below. A map of Bikaner.

11

making themselves suzerains of an arid area called Marwar, now known as Jodhpur.

In 1486 Bika, the second son of the ruler of Jodhpur, started construction on the main fort of his kingdom, Bikaner. It was sited at Rati Ghati, or the Red Pass, a meeting point of desert trade routes. Bika requested the presence of the saint who had blessed him, Karniji, now to bestow her blessings on his citadel. This she consented to do, and attended a solemn ceremony to dignify Bika's bastion. For her blessings, which had crowned Bika's endeavours with victory, Karniji was revered by Bika's descendants as the guardian deity of their dynasty. Three years later Bika founded a city by his fort which was named after himself – Bikaner, the city of Bika.

Bika's courage in braving the hostilities of nature, in quelling the warring inhabitants of the territories he conquered, in holding at bay the ambitions of neighbouring powers and in bringing security to his subjects was proof of his capacity as a ruler. When he died in 1504, leaving ten sons to secure his conquests, all eight of his mourning queens mounted his funeral pyre to perish with their heroic husband.

Bika's son, Lunkaran, followed the martial footsteps of his father, annexing hundreds of villages to the domain of Bikaner. Lunkaran was famous for his charity to his poorer subjects and also for the generous gifts that he made to bards and scholar-priests. During his reign Bikaner became known for its civilised court and for the proud chieftains who came to his gilded audience hall to swear fealty. Lunkaran ended his days on the battlefield trying to extend his territories even further. His forces clashed with the defending army of the Nawab of Narnaul a few miles outside the latter's capital. The Italian historian Tessitori describes Lunkaran's last moment when "like a wounded boar, he throws himself in the middle of

The heirlooms most prized by the Bikaner dynasty date back to the 5th century and the first Rathore Kingdom of Kanauj. These emblems consist of an idol of the family goddess, the sandalwood throne of their Kanauj ancestors, the state umbrella, a diamond-studded shield, a sword, dagger, war drum and lesser royal insignia. Formerly the heirlooms had been the proud possessions of the Rathores of Marwar, and were housed securely in the fort at Jodhpur.

Above. The proud motto on the Bikaner coat-of-arms in Hindi letters is Jai Jangaldhar Badshah – "Victory to the King of the Desert." It was during the reign of Queen Victoria that the Indian rulers adopted the European style for crests.

Below. A painting of the heirlooms and state regalia of the Rathore dynasty of Bikaner.

the enemy army and falls transfixed by a hundred spears."

By the 16th century the whole of Hindustan had been conquered by the Great Moghuls, and their empire brought a golden epoch to India's history. In the early days of Moghul conquest the kings of Bikaner resisted the new power, knowing their kingdom's salvation lay in the desert. No army could sustain a long campaign in its scorching sands. Indeed, when the first Moghul Emperor, Babur, sent his son at the head of a large army to conquer Bikaner, the exhausted Moghul troops were soundly defeated at the village of Chotariya by Bikaner's ruler, Jaitsi. The imperial forces fled, abandoning even the regal umbrella which shaded their Moghul prince's head. That umbrella is preserved to this day at the village where the battle took place, a proud memento of the Rathore victory.

Within two generations the Moghul empire had eschewed war for diplomacy in dealing with the fiercely independent kings of Rajputana, and Bikaner's rulers made peace with the emperors. Rai Singh of Bikaner served Akbar, the Great Moghul, becoming one of his ablest generals. He distinguished himself in the campaign in Gujarat and during the assault on the city of Ahmedabad, Rai Singh killed its rebellious governor, Mirza Mohammad Hussain, in single combat.

Rai Singh's brother, Prithiviraj – popularly known as Peethal – was renowned for his brilliant poems as well as his valour. Indeed, he was one of the legendary nine human gems – philosophers, artists, scholars – who adorned the court of the Great Moghul, and on his death the distressed emperor composed the epitaph:
With Peethal gone,
Gone the attractions of the Majlis,
Gone the pleasure of assembly,
Gone the gathering of friends.

Above left. *The gateway to the Karni Mata Temple. On this temple dedicated to Karniji, Bikaner's grateful maharajas lavished marble gates, silver doors and a gold canopy. Karniji had blessed the founder of their dynasty, Bika, when he set out to carve a kingdom for himself.*

Above right. *The cenotaphs of the Bikaner rulers in the desert at*

Devikund Sagar, a few miles outside Bikaner City. Ganga Singh was cremated here like so many of his ancestors.

Below. *The sandalwood throne from Kanauj. This ancient heirloom of the Bikaner dynasty was only recovered after Rao Bika had waged war successfully against his younger brother, Rao Sujoji, the ruler of Jodhpur.*

Opposite. Seth Chand Mal Dhada's haveli. The seths, or merchants, of Bikaner lived in fine havelis or mansions. These opulent houses were built along narrow lanes to prevent the direct glare of the sun falling upon them. The interiors contained three courtyards – one for the men to gather, another to assure women their privacy, and the third adorned with idols of deities worshipped by the family. The passages or verandahs that surrounded each courtyard served as refreshing air corridors during the heat of summer.

Above. Junagadh Fort seen from Sursagar Lake. Junagadh, meaning "old fort" in Hindi, is considered one of India's most impressive citadels.

Below. The Laxmi Niwas wing of Lallgarh Palace, named after Ganga Singh's father, Maharaja Lal Singh. This new red sandstone palace was laid out with formal gardens filled with English flowers and shade trees.

accompanied by the musicians who played the great war drums – the nagaras. When his son built the beautiful Laxmi Nathji Temple, singers and musicians from distant religious centres were invited to perform at the temple. Within one generation the kingdom of Bikaner had already gained a reputation as a magnet for the arts. At the time of the Great Moghuls, Bikaner's singers performed before the emperors, and imperial musicians visited Bikaner's court.

Under the patronage of civilised monarchs, culture flourished at the Bikaner court. Poets, story-tellers, scholars and writers were rewarded handsomely for their work. Old Rajasthani literature was chronicled by historians so that it could be saved for posterity. Schools of painting evolved, particularly between the 16th and 18th centuries. Master artists from the imperial court at Delhi and great painters from the Deccan kingdoms of the south came to Bikaner and left their influence. As the era of early wars passed, palaces and temples proliferated in Bikaner, and the paintings captured the pleasure of life at that time with their themes of kings and queens, royal courts, hunts, love scenes, gardens and musical entertainments.

DUNGAR SINGH

The Emperor Aurangseb passed away at the beginning of the 18th century. His death signalled the gradual eclipse of Moghul power as ambitious kings fought for supremacy in the impotence of a once-mighty empire. Bikaner's maharajas tried to keep their kingdom intact in spite of intrigues at court, disaffection among local nobles and attacks by marauding armies, but the anarchy of the times led to the slow decline of Bikaner's prosperity. Still, because of its remote geographical position

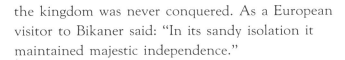

Above. *The main building at Mayo College.*

Below. *Maharaja Gangha Singh between Sir Charles and Lady Bayley. Sir Charles acted as president of the Regency Council of Bikaner for three years during Ganga Singh's minority.*

Opposite. *From left to right: Maharaja Dungar Singh, his father Maharaja Lal Singh and his young brother Ganga Singh. As Sandar Singh had no heirs, his cousin Dungar Singh succeeded him to the throne. Dungar Singh's father, Lal Singh, advised him wisely during his short reign. Ganga Singh succeeded his elder brother at the early age of seven.*

the kingdom was never conquered. As a European visitor to Bikaner said: "In its sandy isolation it maintained majestic independence."

For a century, war and instability reigned where once the writ of the Moghul emperors had run. By the beginning of the 19th century another power had seized the mantle of the Moghul Empire – Great Britain. The ruler of Bikaner, Surat Singh, besieged by defiant nobles and with the warring Pindaris at the borders of his kingdom, in desperation sent emissaries to Lord Hastings, the British Governor General, to negotiate a protective alliance. In 1818 Bikaner signed a treaty with the East India Company in which both sides pledged "Perpetual friendship, alliance and a unity of interests," and British troops entered Bikaner to quell the insurrection of the Maharaja's rebellious thakurs, or barons.

The protection of the British now secured external and internal peace for the state. For their part, Bikaner's rulers came to the support of the British in their times of trouble. During the Second Sikh war in 1848, a body of horse and artillery was provided by the state to fight for the British. In the Afghan War of 1842 camels were supplied for the Kabul Expedition. And during the Great Uprising of 1857 against British power, Maharaja Sardar Singh raised a strong force which marched to support the beleaguered Englishmen.

Inevitably, the long years of internal strife coupled with the necessity to come to the military and financial aid of its new ally, the British, had devastated the revenues of the kingdom. The treasury was in debt. A large and mostly untrained army, still maintained for the sake of old-fashioned traditions, swallowed up vast sums of public money. There were no schools or hospitals, and regular administration hardly existed.

Maharaja Ganga Singh with his tutor, Pandit Ram Chandra Dubey, on his left. The young Maharaja was deeply attached to his Hindi teacher, and with good reason, since the excellent grounding he received in Indian subjects placed him in good stead both as a ruler and later as chancellor of one of India's leading educational institutions, the Banaras Hindu University.

Opposite. The main hall at Mayo College, Ajmer. This fabled institution was described by a British educator as "the Eton of the East". Modelled after Britain's public schools, young princes of royal India were given a Western education with Imperialist overtones and were prepared to be rulers of their states. The princes often had their own residences – Bikaner House was built for Ganga Singh – and they lived with their retainers and private tutors while following the college's curriculum. Mayo College still exists today as a school for India's upper classes.

It was during the reign of Maharaja Dungar Singh, who succeeded Sardar Singh, that Bikaner made its transition from a land bankrupted by costly military adventures to one properly run by a civil administration. In 1875 Dungar Singh, a youth of eighteen years, was consecrated as the new Maharaja of Bikaner. Almost immediately he undertook a religious pilgrimage, and during his journey he travelled through several provinces which were under British rule. Deeply impressed by the progress he saw, Dungar Singh was inspired to modernise Bikaner.

Dungar Singh reformed Bikaner's land revenues from an archaic and ineffectual system to a more efficient one of direct payment to the state. Bikaner was divided into comprehensive districts, each administered by well-trained officials. Regular courts of law, modelled on the courts in British India, and a newly formed police force were successful in checking rampant lawlessness. Hospitals were founded and education was made free throughout the state. Revenue yielding schemes were initiated, and this, added to the conservation of finances, increased the revenues of the state. Maharaja Dungar Singh was also the first Indian ruler to introduce electricity to his kingdom, as early as 1886.

By the time Dungar Singh died in 1887 he had firmly laid the foundation for his kingdom's entry into the 20th century, an achievement acknowledged by his subjects in a monument raised to him.

GANGA SINGH

It was the kingdom of Bikaner's good fortune that the enlightened Maharaja Dungar Singh was succeeded by an even more brilliant ruler – his younger brother, Ganga Singh. As Dungar Singh

Maharaja Ganga Singh, like the rulers of other Princely Indian States such as Patiala, Kashmir, Jodhpur and Bhopal, maintained his own polo team. He competed with the teams of those maharajas and with British officers of the Indian Army. Polo had been popular in India since Moghul times when Imperial princes were known to have played the game even late into the night, using luminous balls coated in sulphur from the sea. In the mid-19th century, Englishmen laid out the rules for polo in their clubs in Eastern India – rules which are followed by all polo players to this day.

Above. Young Ganga Singh ready for a chukka of polo.

Below. Ganga Singh riding in the desert.

Opposite. Maharaja Ganga Singh, in his twenties, with the Bikaner Polo Team.

had no sons, this brother had from birth lived in the royal apartment at Junagadh Fort, his education supervised by the ruler and his parents.

In Panikkar's biography, we are informed of the first moments of the new Maharaja's reign :

"The young prince was hardly seven years old when Maharaja Dungar Singhji passed away in the prime of his life. It was a warm August evening and the boy, without a care in the world, was playing with his companions in one of the shaded courtyards of the palace. His game was interrupted by the sudden appearance of two venerable court dignitaries whose gravity of mien announced that something serious had happened. The important thing was to get the boy changed into suitable clothes for he was, as usual, clad in bright-coloured clothes with gold braid. With practised tact the prince was wheedled to his suite of apartments and persuaded to change into more sober clothes, and led away to accept the homage of his people."

On his coronation Ganga Singh was ushered to the throne room where he did obeisance to the traditional Singhasan or throne of his ancestors. Then the premier nobles of the land raised him to the throne as 121 guns thundered a salute, informing the people of Bikaner they had a new Rathore ruler, the twenty-first of his line.

Being only seven years old, Ganga Singh was unable to govern his kingdom. The government was conducted in his name by a Council of Regency. The Political Agent of the British Empire was its president. All members of the Regency Council were nominated and approved by the empire's Political Department.

The Regency Council attempted to continue some of the reforms initiated by Maharaja Dungar Singh. Land revenue settlements were revised and an effort was made to open the country to the railways. However, the constant fear remained

The birth of a royal son was an event of great rejoicing as it assured the continuation of the dynasty. Maharaja Ganga Singh married the princess of Pratapgarh aged 17. She is not seen in the pictures as high-born indian ladies maintained purdah. Above left is Ganga Singh holding Prince Sadul Singh and above right he holds his daughter princess Chand Kanwar. The daughter fell ill during World War I and died, while the son lived on to become the last crowned ruler of Bikaner. Opposite are the two children in all their finery.

that officials nominated by the British Raj would barter away the rights of a ruler and the independent status of the state. Furthermore, many of the reforms begun by Maharaja Dungar Singh stagnated during the days of the regency. Indeed, in the absence of an adult sovereign, corruption went unchecked and intrigues multiplied, giving credence to the saying, "it bodes ill for a kingdom when it is ruled by a child."

At the end of the regency, the construction of the new Lallgarh Palace began on the outskirts of Bikaner city. The magnificent Junagadh fort, which had been the residence of Bikaner's monarchs for 400 years, was now considered too unwieldy a group of buildings for an Occidental way of life, since the British Raj desired Oriental rulers to become Anglicised gentlemen.

As for Ganga Singh, his education was placed in the competent hands of Pandit Ram Chandra Dubey, a fine teacher of Indian history, culture and languages, who taught the Maharaja the necessity of keeping close contacts with his own people and grounded him in a deep knowledge of his state's history and customs. Ganga Singh's early education was to stand him in good stead, and at the age of nine the Regency Council decided to send him to be educated at a "modern" British establishment for young princes and chiefs, the Mayo College at Ajmer.

For the next five years Ganga Singh was trained in those accomplishments the British considered essential for an Indian prince, which were enumerated by a British educationalist as: "the speaking of faultless English, possesing excellent table manners, and playing good cricket." By the time Ganga Singh left Mayo College, where he was a star pupil, he was proficient in many British sports and subjects.

On his return to Bikaner, the young ruler needed to be trained in administrative affairs. For

Maharaja Ganga Singh often travelled to Europe to render homage to his King Emperor and to represent India at important international conferences.

Opposite. A session of the League of Nations Assembly in Geneva, September 1930, in which Maharaja Ganga Singh led the Indian delegation.

Above. The Maharaja sails to England for the coronation of Edward VII.

Below. The Maharaja's close friend, George V, in the uniform of the British Indian Army.

this purpose the Government of India chose an Englishman, Brian Egerton, as his tutor. Egerton was impressed by this young charge. "While His Highness was assiduous in his studies, his activity was amazing. Riding and shooting before breakfast and study morning and afternoon, polo in the evening, and at a later date, roller skating to finish up with was an ordinary day's routine, varied on holidays by a ride out eighteen miles to Gajner, shooting and pig-sticking there, and riding back in time for polo in the afternoon. . . . During the few years of my tutorship I had seen His Highness develop into a tall young man of striking appearance, a brilliant polo player, a marvellous shot, a keen pig-sticker and a perfect host."

By the time Ganga Singh was seventeen years old, the Regency Council decided he was old enough to be married and duly arranged a match with the young Princess of Pratapgarh. Horoscopes were exchanged; more important, dowries were negotiated, and the wedding was celebrated with great splendour in July 1887.

In the following year the young Maharaja gained his majority and assumed full ruling powers at a formal ceremony held at Junagadh Fort. Now Ganga Singh was faced with the realities of ruling a state. Panikkar writes: "He knew the proud heritage of Rao Bikaji which had descended to him was not for one whose ideal was that of having an easy time. The state of Bikaner with its area of 23,000 square miles, with its complex interests, conditions, and problems, its isolated position, its scarcity and precarious rainfall, its restless populace, and its proud and untamed aristocracy, required constant vigilance and unceasing activity. His state was not rich. . . . Though its mineral wealth was great, it was underdeveloped; though much of its area was fertile, there was neither adequate rainfall nor irrigation to enable the ryots to cultivate the land. The vast area over which he ruled was unconnected with the capital except by primitive methods of transport. To a young Maharaja, active, enthusiastic, and with visions of future greatness for his country, there was little time for ease or for pleasure. Nor indeed was the Maharaja even given a chance of taking his duties lightly."

The opportunity for Ganga Singh to prove his good intentions came tragically soon. Within six months of his assuming ruling powers the whole of Northern India was laid waste by famine as the monsoon rains failed. For Bikaner the drought was a catastrophe. There had been scarcely any rain in the previous three years, and the Regency Council had been unable to make sufficient preparations for a famine. The grain stores of the state lay empty and starving villagers deserted their parched fields, leaving their livestock to perish.

The Maharaja, still only in his teens, immediately appointed a famine committee and involved himself completely in the programme of distributing food grain to the needy and work for the poor. Journeying by camel or horseback, in the company of a handful of officials, Ganga Singh toured his dominions trying to bring succour to his subjects. To avoid epidemics, medical camps were set up. Loans were given to villagers who needed money to replace the cattle they had lost. The unflagging efforts of Ganga Singh during the famine won him admiration from the Viceroy of India, Lord Curzon, who said the Maharaja was "his own famine officer throughout that fearful time and conducted his campaign with indefatigable energy and skill." In recognition of Ganga Singh's endeavours Queen Victoria conferred on him the Kaiser-i-Hind gold medal.

Above. "Some Statesmen of the Great War", painted by Sir James Guthrie. National Portrait Gallery, London. Ganga Singh is standing by the pillar on the extreme left.

Opposite. King George V and Queen Mary were extremely friendly with Ganga Singh, and they visited each other on numerous occasions. Here are the King and Queen in India in 1911 with several maharajas. Ganga Singh is on the far right.

The Maharaja's exposure to his people during the forays he made deep into his state at the time of the famine gave him a first-hand knowledge of their needs. Because of the horrors he had witnessed, and having observed so closely the suffering of his people, he resolved "that never again, if human enterprise and skill can prevent it, shall Bikaner face such a situation."

Within a year the young Maharaja was called to lead his troops against the Dowager Empress of China during the Boxer Rebellion – the first of three wars in three continents which he fought overseas for the British Empire. The Maharaja's courage and discipline were mentioned in despatches and he was highly decorated for his martial endeavours in all the campaigns in which he took part.

During the Great War the Maharaja of Bikaner and his troops served in Flanders and in Egypt. The Maharaja represented his fellow rulers at the meetings of the Imperial War Cabinet held in England in 1917, 1918 and 1919. He was one of the signatories to the Treaty of Versailles concluded between the Allied Forces and the newly formed German Republic, which ended the Great War. Although he was honoured to sign such a historic document on behalf of his country's forces, the Maharaja stated publicly "that such a treaty which imposed such burdens upon the vanquished enemy could not be the harbinger of a lasting peace."

In 1918 Bikaner's Maharaja was invited as one of the plenipotentiaries to the Peace Conference which was held in Paris, and presided over by President Clémenceau, President Wilson and Prime Minister Lloyd George. Here Ganga Singh and the other Indian representative, Lord Sinha, argued most forcefully for the inclusion of India in the newly formed League of Nations. Ignoring British opinion and pressure, Ganga Singh said

"The League should be open to every civilised nation. . . . I would beg to point out that on this ground alone the claim of India for inclusion in the League of Nations is unimpeachable." He won the day, and India became a member of the League, leading Lloyd George to remark "We soon found out that he was one of the Wise Men that came from the East."

While playing his part on the world stage, Ganga Singh also set himself the task of developing to the full the state's resources and institutions by incorporating the best ideas from the West and East. The Viceroy, Lord Minto, noted that "the Maharaja, while recognising what is good in Western ways of thought, has not allowed himself to become disassociated from the religion, the tradition and the individuality of his own countrymen."

In pursuit of this ambition the Maharaja built a well-knit and efficient system of railways, which connected every corner of the state with its capital. He quadrupled the roads within the dominion. Ambitious waterworks and electrical schemes were undertaken in the important towns, and he took on the task of the industrialisation of Bikaner. Coal mines, cotton ginning mills, wool-press factories, glass works, soap factories and printing presses brought prosperity to the people and multiplied the state's revenues.

The single most important contribution the Maharaja made to the state was the building of the 89-mile-long Gang Canal, bringing water from the rivers of the Punjab to his desert kingdom. Having experienced the tragedy of the famine of 1899, Ganga Singh had spent the next three decades in convincing the British Government to lend their support to his dream of making his country fertile and of raising funds to make this dream possible. His perseverance finally led, in 1927, to the opening of the biggest concrete-lined

Opposite. *King George V riding with his honorary aide-de-camp, Ganga Singh, in London in 1919, shortly after the Great War. The British royal family shared with India's maharajas a passion for horses.*

Above. *King George V's heir, the Prince of Wales, visits Bikaner in 1921 with his equerry, Captain "Fruity" Metcalfe. In his memoirs, the Prince — then the Duke of Windsor — remembered his trip to India as one of the happiest experiences of his youth. For this visit, a great ceremonial arch was erected for the royal party to pass through, and the Prince pursued all of India's favorite sports — polo, pig sticking and shooting tiger as well as waterfowl.*

canal in the world, which recovered nearly 1,000 square miles from the grip of the desert and made them into a land of flourishing fields.

Maharaja Ganga Singh's extraordinary breadth of vision led him to the realisation that the absolute powers of a feudal monarch were inhibiting the further evolution of his people. His discussions with international statemen and observations of foreign governments convinced him that Bikaner should become a constitutional monarchy. Believing the voice of the people should be heard in a progressive government, the ruler established the Representative Assembly of Bikaner, consisting of elected members, which was inaugurated in 1913.

To ensure true justice the Maharaja felt the law courts should be independent and protected from interference from any arm of the administration. To this end the Maharaja established a high court and a number of lower courts, and separated them from the administration. In 1922 Ganga Singh was the first ruler in Rajputana to grant a full charter of powers to the state's High Court.

But Ganga Singh was fully aware that the granting of rights was meangingless if illiteracy prevented his subjects from taking advantage of them. Passionate about education, Ganga Singh ensured that every important town had a college and every prominent village a school. A trust gave scholarships to those students wishing to pursue further studies outside the state. The Maharaja was a champion of female education in a region of India where girls were thought to be such a financial burden that female infanticide was still practised. He founded schools and colleges for them, including schools for girls who observed purdah, so that they would not lack education.

Indefatigable himself, the Maharaja was a hard taskmaster, sparing neither himself nor his officials

Maharaja Ganga Singh was the foremost spokesman for Princely India, and travelled to many important conferences.

Above. A cartoon of Winston Churchill with several Indian rulers at the first Round Table Conference held in London in 1930 to discuss the future system for governing India. There were representatives from Britain, British India and the Indian States. Ganga Singh is on Churchill's left.

Opposite above. Maharaja Ganga Singh receiving the Freedom of the City of London in 1917. On this occasion he spoke of World War I when Indian and British troops fought side by side."

Opposite below. Ganga Singh in London as a member of the Imperial War Cabinet during World War I.

Overleaf, left. the desert Kingdom of Bikaner suffered a severe drought in 1899. Villagers climb the desert hills to fill their buckets with rationed water and sit in rows awaiting the distribution of grain from the Family Relief Program initiated by Ganga Singh.

Overleaf, right. After the great famine, Ganga Singh built an extensive railway system in his state, which created revenue and carried necessities swiftly to his people during natural catastrophes. A railway engine proudly displays the Bikaner crest in 1912.

during long hours of work. One of his officials said, "He made us work like slaves when he wanted work done on time. I used to come home sometimes at four in the morning and leave again at nine and not see my children for over a fortnight."

Pannikar provides other insights into Ganga Singh's personality. "Essentially a soldier, statesman and administrator, the Maharaja is little moved by the appeal of the arts. . . . His lack of humanistic interest gives the Maharaja a mainly utilitarian outlook on life. . . . and consequently there is a rigidity and inelasticity in his general ideas. It was therefore not by versatility but by concentration on things of immediate interest that the Maharaja achieved greatness."

For relaxation Ganga Singh enjoyed the pleasures of the hunt, usually at the beautiful lake palace he had built at Gajner, some miles away from the city of Bikaner. Here, and at the grand city palace of Lallgarh, he entertained a legion of guests, as described by Iris Butler in *A Viceroy's Wife*: "Sir Ganga Singh. . . . occupied a great position in Indian politics and social life. A man of striking personal beauty, charm and great ambition. . . . A very cosmopolitan, a very sophisticated man, but one who never forgot his Rajput past. He was a wonderful host and did not ignore old friends even if they were quite unimportant people. Neither did he ever fail to keep contact with friends old and new who were very important people. . ."

The most important person Ganga Singh numbered amongst his friends was the King-Emperor of India, George V. On the occasion of Edward VII's coronation Ganga Singh was received by George V, then Prince of Wales. The young Maharaja, with his dashing good looks and cosmopolitan manners, was an immediate success in the first circles of London. Ganga Singh was

appointed Honorary Aide-de-Camp to the Prince of Wales, and the ties of friendship between the two young men were further strengthened when the Prince of Wales visited Bikaner with his wife in 1905. On his departure from the kingdom, Prince George wrote: "I can assure you that among the happy recollections that the Princess and I will carry away from India, none will be more cherished than those of our most enjoyable stay at Bikaner, and of the friendship between you and ourselves which has been so firmly cemented."

After the Prince of Wales assumed the mantle of King-Emperor of India, the close friendship with his A.D.C. continued, and Queen Mary remained especially fond of the Indian ruler. During Ganga Singh's last illness, the widowed Queen often cabled him, pleading that he take his doctor's instructions seriously. She ended her messages with the request: "Do not forget your old friend, Mary."

Another distinguished friend of Ganga Singh's was President Clémenceau, known as the "Tiger of France". The Maharaja first met Clémenceau in 1919 when, as a representative of India, he attended the Peace Conference in Paris. After the signing of the Peace Treaty of Versailles, President Clémenceau resigned from office at the age of seventy-nine. Ganga Singh urged "Le Tigre de France" to visit India and attend a shikar for wild tigers, an invitation which the President accepted in the following year. True to his promise the Maharaja organised a shoot, and the old man bagged two tigers. On his return to France the President wrote, "I see you are not a great writer, but I am not going to complain of it, my reason being that you are as near perfection as imperfection can be. . . . Wherever you are, if you do not write a line I will call you a great prince but a very naughty boy."

Opposite, above and below right. The opening of the Gang Canal, 26 October, 1927. During this occasion, for which Ganga Singh had worked three decades, the Viceroy, Lord Irwin, said in his speech: "Researches, I believe, have shown that centuries ago a river flowed through Bikaner, and that much of what is now a parched and thirsty waste was once a green land of gardens. Long ago it disappeared, and with it went the population of this country in a great emigration to the Indus Valley. It is a strange and happy reversal of fortune that that lost river of the desrt is now being restored to its ancient site, and that once again men will be able to live in comfort and plenty on its plains."

Opposite left. Maharaja Ganga Singh by the Gang Canal in his old age. Years before, at the time of the opening of the canal, Ganga Singh said in his speech: "I have been taught to live for my people, their hopes and aspirations have been my prime ambition, and their well-being my supreme reward."

Overleaf. Indian princes spent a great deal of time visiting each other's kingdoms, and there was a long-standing tradition of reciprocal hospitality. A royal visit was a pretext for sumptuous banquets, entertainments, sport and performances. Left. a state banquet for Maharaja Ganga Singh at the enormous and opulent Laxmi Vilas Palace in Baroda. Ganga Singh's host, Maharaja Sayajirao III, introduced far-reaching social, administrative and educational reforms in his state.

Overleaf. Above right. Maharaja Ganga Singh in a group portrait with the Baroda royal family. Seated on his right is Maharani Chimra Bai, a great believer in the emancipation of women, who did not observe purdah.

Overleaf. Below right. A visit to the Nizam of Hyderabad (sixth from left) reputed to be the richest man in the world. The Aga Khan is third from the right.

During the three decades that Ganga Singh was working tirelessly to make his kingdom into a modern state, the British Raj had increased its interference in the affairs of Royal India. The Raj had encroached so deeply on the treaty rights of the rulers that soon the power of India's kings would be reduced to mere form, while the British Empire acquired the substance of a kingdom's sovereignty.

Ganga Singh, like many other Indian rulers, chafed under the restrictions the British Raj placed on his activities within and outside his state. The Maharaja believed that if the Indian rulers united and put forward their claims, they could stall the erosion of their powers. His efforts led the British Raj to agree to the creation of a Chamber of Princes, which was inaugurated at the Red Fort at Delhi in 1921. Maharaja Ganga Singh was elected by his brother rulers to be its first chancellor, a position he held for a number of years.

The resentment in Royal India against the interference of the British Raj was infinitely more pronounced in British India, where the nationalist movement was engulfing its imperial masters. Ganga Singh's loyalty to the British Empire over three wars did not colour his enlightened views on liberty for British India or subdue his admiration for those men of courage who fought for their nation's freedom.

The Maharaja advocated Home Rule and counted among his friends nationalist leaders like Mahatma Gandhi and Rabindranath Tagore, the Nobel Prize Laureate.

In 1933 Maharaja Ganga Singh and his wife Maharani Bhatianji Sahira celebrated their Silver Wedding Anniversay. The Maharani maintained purdah, and at the time of the anniversary Ganga Singh spoke of her in public for the first time. The Maharani took a particular interest in increasing the number of hospitals within the state

as well as the number of schools and colleges for women. For her outstanding work, she was one of the few women to receive from the British Empire the highly prized Crown of India decoration.

The year 1937 was the fiftieth anniversary of Maharaja Ganga Singh's accession to the throne. To honour this event the people of Bikaner held tremendous celebrations for his Golden Jubilee. The festivities and ceremonies were seemingly endless in a city hung with banners proclaiming "Long Live our Maharaja" and "Silver leads to Gold leads to Diamond." There were religious ceremonies at the temples, elephant and camel processions, military tournaments and torchlit tattoos, state durbars and audiences, banquets for distinguished visitors and Bikaner's nobility, fireworks, fairs, and musical performances that went on all night.

To mark the occasion, the Maharaja waived loans to farmers and raised the pay of the state's employees and armed forces. More hospitals and schools were opened and the Golden Jubilee Museum was inaugurated. The people of Bikaner weighed Ganga Singh in gold, confident that their sovereign would use this treasure for their benefit. At the end of the year, when all the celebrations had been concluded, Bikaner continued to have an air of unreality. It took some time for the people of Bikaner to resume their normal lives after their city and state had been the scene of so much festivity and splendour.

With the coming of World War II Ganga Singh, who now held the status of full general in the British Army, offered to go to the front. When told that his age stood in the way, the Maharaja declared that "No Rajput is too old to fight at the age of sixty." In 1941, accompanied by his grandson, he proceeded on active service to the Middle East. He returned to India within the year and a few months later was diagnosed with

Above. *The Bikaner Camel Corps.*

Opposite. *An elephant fight during Ganga Singh's visit to Udaipur. These fights between male tuskers took place during the mating period. A low wall separated the elephants that knocked their foreheads against each other and lashed out with their trunks. If the fight became too violent, the elephants were separated by means of spears and sticks.*

cancer. The illness did not prevent Ganga Singh from working to the end on a huge new irrigation project to benefit his kingdom. Perhaps it is only fitting that the last words of Bikaner's great Maharaja were "Get me the Bhakra Dam file."

Ganga Singh was cremated at the cenotaphs of his ancestors while newspapers around the world carried his obituaries. The *Times of India* wrote of his "fine record of heroic and paramount achievement for a major part of his sixty-three years, devoted with single-mindedness to the service of his people and his country. In so doing he placed Bikaner on the map and himself became a figure of world distinction."

Ganga Singh's daughter, the Maharani of Kotah, recalls in *The Lives of the Indian Princes*: "When my father used to come for dinner, sometimes we were allowed to sit there with him. He would have his pencil and chit-pads and while eating, he would write with his left hand, making notes and we thought it was wonderful, sharpening his pencils and thinking that we were great office bearers."

It was fortunate for Bikaner that Ganga Singh himself trained his children in administration and the art of government because the brief reign of his son, Maharaja Sadul Singh, was to prove the most painful period in Bikaner's history.

On the eve of its departure, the British Empire partitioned the subcontinent into the two nations of India and Pakistan, unleashing a civil war of unparalleled savagery. But history records that no blood was spilled at the borders that Bikaner shared with Pakistan because of the military precautions taken by Maharaja Sadul Singh. More sinister for Bikaner's future was the imminent danger of the British gifting to Pakistan the water source that fed the Gang Canal. An agitated Maharaja Sadul Singh, realising that his state was on the verge of reverting to the desert, battled

with the Viceroy and the ministers at Delhi to reverse the decision. This he succeeded in doing and with this last great act of statesmanship, protected his people's future prosperity.

In 1949 it was Maharaja Sadul Singh's mournful duty to preside over the demise of his kingdom, as Bikaner was integrated into the Union of a free India. Recognising the historical imperative of the times, Sadul Singh was intrumental in persuading many Indian rulers to join the Union voluntarily in order to prevent civil wars and further bloodshed. On his death in 1950, the first President of the Republic of India paid tribute to Sadul Singh's contribution to peace in the subcontinent with the words, "India is, and will remain, indebted to him."

His father's realism and devotion to his people's interests left a deep impression on Karni Singh, the first ruler of Bikaner to be anointed Maharaja in a democracy. Refusing to live in the

Above. Maharaja Sadul Singh with Pandit Jawaharlal Nehru, the Republic of India's first Prime Minister.

Below. Maharaja Sadul Singh with Sardar Vallabhbhai Patel, who was known as "The Iron Man of India". Patel was responsible for the integration of the Princely States into the Union of India. Opposite, from right to left. Prince Sadul Singh with his sons Karni Singh and Amar Singh.

past, Karni Singh entered active politics and ran for parliament in the first Indian general election.

Karni Singh often told the story that as a child, whenever he asked his grandfather, Maharaja Ganga Singh, to stop working and play with his grandchildren, Ganga Singh replied ruefully, "I cannot stop working. I have to earn my salary."

Both a crack shot who represented India at several Olympics and an avid wild-life preservationist who made the royal shooting grounds into a famous wild-life preserve, Maharaja Kurni Singh was a philanthropist who converted his private holdings into charitable trusts. But perhaps Karni Singh's proudest claim would have been that, elected to office for five consecutive terms, he too for over a quarter of a century could have been said to have "earned his salary" in the service of the people of Bikaner.

LIFE IN BIKANER

For a hundred years, until the middle of the 19th century, Bikaner was at the mercy of many lawless thakurs, or landlords. They ran the countryside in defiance of their maharaja, and no one seemed able to check their plundering, as is evident from a description in Powlett's *Gazetteer*:

"Every one who has the means possesses a small fort which is surrounded by a rampart of sand... and within it are usually found more houses than the ostensible means of the owner justify his keeping. When a dacoity at some distant point is contemplated the thakur gives his horses a daily allowance of ghee (clarified butter) for some time previously in order to fit them for extraordinary exertion, and then, banded with some active neighbours, they make a long night journey, often guided by the stars, to the spot which they wish to reach. Here, till the arrival of the victims, they will lie hidden under a mound or a thin hedge. The booty, which usually consists of camels and their burdens, including perhaps the wife of a rich bania (trader), is then hurried off without delay."

While the men toiled in the fields, the village women went about their daily chores: drawing precious water from deep wells, sitting in earthen huts grinding grain while their infants slumbered in cloth hammocks by their side, or preparing for their husbands and sons a midday meal of the simple fare of local farmers: millet bread, curds and red chili. They wove fabrics in bright colours for their daughters' dowries, and stitched appliquéd quilts to be used on winter nights when biting winds came blowing down from the dune-like hillocks of the desert.

Their languid sisters in the city did not believe in exertion. They spent hours gossiping in rooms shaded

Inset. *A colorfully dressed village woman.*

Opposite. *A group of thakurs of Bikaner. Like their ruler, thakurs were of the Rathore clan, whose ancestors had accompanied the founder of the kingdom, Rao Bika, on his search for a state. Others belonged to different Rajput clans who came to seek service at the Bikaner court. They made up the state's aristocracy.*

by latticed screens, all the while nibbling silver-coated sweet meats and bhujia — a spicy lentil-based savoury particular to Bikaner. Their lives of leisure gave credence to an old saying about the prosperity of the city:

For her camels and her men of wealth,
For her ornamented sweets and her ornaments of gold
And the supreme beauty of her women,
For these five treasures
Is Bikaner famed.

Meanwhile turbaned villagers scratched out a frugal existence, under the merciless desert sun, ploughing fields which barely supported such hardy crops as millet and gum. Meagre herds of cattle, sheep and goats were their only wealth, although more fortunate villagers sometimes owned a camel, the natural mount of the desert, and the occasional horse.

Even the rich seths, or merchants of the trading community, who controlled the commerce of the capital and extended their trade to distant regions of India, were at the mercy of robber barons from the moment their caravans left the protection of the city walls. And in the city itself, it was not safe to go abroad at night except in the company of armed guards.

It was during the reign of Ganga Singh that the thakurs of Bikaner finally ended their feuding. Many of them took responsible positions in the administration, the army and other public walks of life. Maharaja Ganga Singh improved the city of Bikaner so that it now had wide avenues, fine parks and impressive public buildings, but above all he made the city safe for its inhabitants.

Havelis, or mansions, of Bikaner's
seths or merchants

Inset. The formal English Gardens
in the Bikaner Public Park.

Opposite. Another group of
thakurs. Many of these local barons
had broken out in open rebellion
against their maharajas in the 19th
century and were notorious
throughout the land as plunderers.
It was only at the turn of the
present century that they gave up
these pursuits and served the
kingdom as administrators and
officers.

Left. A merchant's wife in
traditional ivory bangles, silver
anklets and toe-rings that denote
her status as a married woman.
The veil and skirts she wears are
made of tie-and-dye-colored cotton.
Above. Two city girls, probably
dancers, in their gossamer veils and
delicate ornaments.

Opposite. A thakur, sitting on a platform, keeps cool in the waters of a rarely filled lake as he is entertained by dancers and musicians.

Above. Wrestling was a popular sport in the Bikaner countryside, as were camel races and a game called Hathdara, similar to cricket, played with string balls and sticks.

Below. A fakir dances on a platform of swords to the accompaniment of a band in a courtyard of Junagadh Fort, while others play religious music on their long-stringed instruments.

Inset. Bikaner musicians.

The dromedary, or single-humped camel, is the friend of the man of the desert. Camel's wool is used to make the shawls, blankets and tents needed in the cold desert nights, and camel's milk serves in lieu of a cow's. The dromedary is used on long journeys to carry its master or his produce, because as a creature of the desert, the camel requires little water over lengthy distances. In arid Bikaner, the creature is equipped today, as in the past, with a crude wooden saddle if it belongs to a peasant, or with embroidered silks if it belongs to a man of status.

Above. Villagers with a camel cart used to bring crops to Bikaner City's market.

Below. Two villagers in the desert with their camels.

Opposite. Travellers watering their dromedaries at a rare pond in an oasis.

Inset. Two camel drivers.

When the harsh summer sun scorches the people of Bikaner, the local craftsmen, weavers and artisans huddle indoors to sculpt, to stitch and sew, to adorn and embellish the local materials available to them in a hostile climate. They create implements of utility whose delicacy and colours adorn the starkness of a desert landscape.

Above. Village women spin woollen yarn. From this were woven the brilliantly colored rough blankets essential to comfort in the freezing desert nights.

Below. Silversmiths making delicate jewelry popular in the city markets.

Inset. A craftsman completes a traditional Bikaner lacquer bangle.

Above. Tailors embroidering fine muslins to be fashioned into full skirts and veils on women's, as well as men's, turbans and tunics.

Below. Bikaner's artisans preparing a lacquer screen bordered with gold leaf and designs in mirror and gesso. The screens decorate the interiors of havelis.

Inset. An overseer smokes his hubble-bubble while observing two stonemasons chisel blocks of red sandstone quarried in the desert.

PALACES, OLD AND NEW

Raja Rai Singh, the sixth Rathore ruler of Bikaner, built the fort of Junagadh. Traditional belief held that a human being should be killed and his corpse buried in the fort's foundation to make the citadel invincible. Consequently, a man was sacrificed in 1588 to mark the commencement of the construction of Junagadh Fort. The massive towers and walls of the fort contained secret armouries and passages so narrow that they could be defended by a single warrior: through the centuries the Suraj Pol, or Gateway of the Sun, the citadel's main entrance, witnessed armies led by Bikaner's kings ride out to war and glory, and never once endured the indignity of conquering forces.

In the fort's durbar, or hall of audience, with its soaring sandstone columns crowned with carvings of elephants, swans and lotus flowers, sat the ruler of Bikaner on his gaddi — the traditional cushioned throne of Indian kings. From the gaddi the maharaja issued daily commands to the assembled ministers, generals and courtiers in matters relating to the governance of the kingdom. Behind the ruler stood two staff-bearers holding the symbols of monarchy: peacock

View from an archway of a courtyard in the Lallgarh Palace. A peacock takes a refreshing sip of water from the pool on a hot summer's day. The scalloped arches that support the verandahs of this courtyard have a peacock motif.

Opposite. A view of Junagadh Fort. The fort-complexes of India were a world within themselves. Besides serving as the residence of the ruler, they were the seat of his court and the center of administration for the state.

feathers and a white horse's tail falling from a golden cone, signs of war and conquest. Other retainers held the Maharaja's ceremonial sword and shield; the former the symbol of implacable justice, the latter displayed so that the people would be aware of their sovereign as protector.

Never ravaged by war, the palaces and pleasure pavilions that proliferated within the forbidding exterior of Junagadh fort bore testimony to the luxuries of peace. Sequestered from the royal public building where the men conducted the affairs of state, the ladies of the harem lived in beautifully painted private quarters. Their apartments were covered with frescoes of religious or poetic themes in gold-leaf, mirror and gesso work, so that each room resembled an exquisitely enamelled casket. Bearing romantic names such as Phool Mahal, the Palace of Flowers, or Chand Mahal, the Palace of the Moon, the apartments were oases of art in a desert. For example, the ceiling of one perfectly preserved room is painted with swollen storm clouds and shafts of lightning. During a time when Bikaner was suffering seven years of drought, the fresco was

Above. *This passage in Junagadh Fort, worked over in lacquer and mirror ornamentation, is amongst many in the maze of corridors within the zenana quarters of the fort. The occupants of the zenana wielded much influence over their royal menfolk from behind the purdah, a Hindi word meaning "curtain". The building activity of such aesthetically designed rooms began in the last decade of the 16th century and continued until early in this century, covering a span of more than four hundred years. All of Bikaner's major rulers altered existing structures, their instructions being realized by gifted architects and master builders, who added further lustre to the palaces within the fort. Over the centuries the earlier buildings changed completely, thus making them a riddle for any historian attempting to organize these edifices in chronological order.*

Below. *Anup Mahal at Junagadh Fort. Anup Singh (reigned 1669-1698) was a contemporary of the last great Moghul Emperor, Aurangzeb, after whose death Imperial power began its decline. The courts of Rajputana, who had patronized the refined arts of the Moghul court, now became the heirs of its disintegrating civilization. Many refugee artists and master craftsmen found sanctuary in the Rajput kingdoms. The Usta artists who came from the Moghul cities of Delhi, Agra and Lahore, contributed a great deal to the artistic excellence of Junagadh Fort.*

Opposite. *The Durbar Hall in Junagadh Fort. Carved superbly by the craftsmen of Bikaner, this hall with its sandstone walls and apricot wood ceiling was one of the rooms viewed by the architects Lutyens and Baker in 1914 when they were touring India to seek designs for building Delhi, the new capital of India.*

Opposite. Hundreds of masons laboured for four years to complete Lallgarh Palace. Huge rocks of red sandstone were quarried from mines in the Thar Desert for the building. Work began in the last year of Ganga Singh's minority, and was paid for by the profits from the railways and the coal mines that the young Maharaja established. By the turn of this century, the rigours of travelling by camel or elephant were a thing of the past. The pachyderm had been replaced by the mechanical elephants of the Occident – a fleet of which can be seen here outside the new palace.

Above. A guest drawing room at Lallgarh Palace. Luxuriously appointed Victorian rooms catered to every comfort as far as European guests were concerned. Omitting the Oriental arches, pillars and windows – and the climate – these rooms could belong to a grand house in England.

Below. a guest bedroom in Lallgarh Palace in 1905. The carpet below the brass bed was made by the interns of Bikaner Jail, who were well known for their superb weaves and design.

SHIKAR
THE SPORT OF MAHARAJAS

The one relaxation Maharaja Ganga Singh, a crack shot, permitted himself was the pleasure of the hunt – shikar. In the state of Bikaner there was little big game, so for hunting lion, tiger, bear and bison, the Maharaja was the honoured guest of rulers in whose jungles such game abounded, or of other high officials in provinces of British India.

In his own kingdom, Maharaja Ganga Singh made his hunting preserve at Gajner legendary for his Imperial Sand Grouse shoot. The grouse was considered a delicacy, but Gajner also offered wild duck, black buck, chinkara, and wild boar.

During the Christmas season, the Imperial Sand Grouse shoot at Gajner was the most sought-after invitation in the Indian social calender. Heads of state, international royalty, Indian rulers, viceroys, and Ganga Singh's personal friends were entertained at week-long house parties at the beautiful palace in Gajner leading down to the lake on which they spent the day in shikar.

Paradoxically, Ganga Singh, while a keen hunter, was avid about conserving wild-life. He introduced different breeds of deer and birds into the state, wild-life preserves were replanted with trees, bush and grass

Opposite. *The Viceroy, Lord Minto, his daughter Lady Eileen Elliot and Lady Minto with Maharaja Ganga Singh seated at the end of a day spent shooting black buck. This buck, after the cheetah, was the fastest animal in India's jungle. The beast could run 50 miles per hour, which made it difficult to shoot.*

Above. *Maharaja Ganga Singh, Lord Minto and party off at dawn for a duck shoot. Gajner Lake, 1908.*

to provide food and shelter for animals, and wardens were posted to see that no poaching took place in the jungle. There was a ban on the hunting of animals during the breeding season, the killing of female animals and their young was strictly prohibited, and anyone caught trapping was severely punished. Enclaves were constructed to protect the animals in their habitat. An illustration of the care given to animals involved a species of Bikaner deer suffering from mineral deficiency. Royal game wardens were instructed to tie slabs of rock salt to the tree trunks so that the deer could lick it and cure themselves.

Ganga Singh's grandson, Maharaja Karni Singh, while sharing his grandfather's encyclopedic knowledge of Bikaner's birds and animals as well as his skill at shooting – he represented India in marksmanship at several Olympic Games – abhorred killing. Karni Singh converted the hunting preserves of Gajner into a wild-life sanctuary and now in the Christmas season, hundreds of visitors crowd the grounds of the hunting palace to watch the Imperial Sand Grouse, wild duck and cranes from distant Siberia drink from the waters of the lake, but the glamour of the brilliant hunting season is gone.

Above. On his European travels, Ganga Singh befriended French President Georges Clémenceau, whom he invited to India. France's "tiger" was interested in hunting his counterpart on the subcontinent. Since there was no big game in Bikaner, Ganga Singh arranged for his guest to shoot tiger at the hunting preserve of the Maharaja of Gwalior. After a day's successful hunting, Clémenceau poses here with Maharaja Ganga Singh on his left and Maharaja Madhar Rao Scindia I of Gwalior on his right. Shivpuri, 1920.

Below. Maharaja Ganga Singh at a lion shoot in the Gir Forest organized by his host the Jam Sahib Digvijay Singh of Nawanagar (right of Ganga Singh). The lion bagged by Ganga Singh lies at his feet.

Opposite and inset. Views of the hunting palace at Gajner, famous in the reign of Ganga Singh and his son Sadul Singh for great shoots and lavish entertainment during the Christmas season. The lush gardens of Gajner were fed by the waters of the lake, and when there was an overflow of guests, splendid tents were set up in the gardens to accommodate them. The park and palace were beautifully lit for lavish dinners and musical entertainments, and a guest later reminisced: "You can't imagine the beauty. It was like 'Arabian Nights' in the desert."

Diner
Potage Fromage
Filets de Pomphret a la Ginois
Imperial Sandgrouse Roti
Plats Bikaner
Pouding a la Marmelade
Café
8-12-43

Shooting waterfowl at Gajner Palace was one of the most prized invitations in India.

Inset. A menu for one of the dinners at the palace.

Above. Shooting practice. Sahibs watch their Mem Sahibs shooting clay pigeons in front of the Junagagdh Palace.

Below. A day's bag of imperial sand grouse in 1949. Yvonne Fitzroy described one such shoot in 1922: "They all sweep down on Gajner for the morning drink. Not in hundreds but in thousands, not for half an hour but for three hours on end. From every direction they come, flying at a tremendous rate in perfect military formation – scouts, vanguard, main body, reinforcements, all complete."

Opposite. The palace at Gajner was built on a man-made lake. This artificial body of water, one of several built by the Maharajas of Bikaner, won the gratitude of despairing farmers in a land of sand and scrub, buffeted by hot winds and layered with dust.

In medieval times, and even earlier, an Indian monarch would demonstrate his prowess in the forest by combatting the tiger, the King of the Jungle, armed merely with bow and arrow. When Europeans arrived in the early 17th century and introduced firearms to India, the sport of tiger shooting became a matter of prestige, and the most exciting hunts were recorded by the numerous fine skins stretched over the walls of a Maharaja's trophy hall.

Opposite. A tiger shot by Maharaja Ganga Singh being rowed across the Chambal River. Kota State, 1930.

Maharaja Ganga Singh awaiting a lion on a machan or wooden platform in the Gir Forest in 1940. Lions were generally shot from these platforms or from elephants. Both methods required beaters to drive the kill towards the hunters. Sometimes hundreds of villagers would take part in this exercise.

Maharaja Ganga Singh with his host, the Jam Sahib Digvijay Singh of Nawanagar (seated at Maharaja Ganga Singh's left) picnicking in the Gir Forest in 1940 while on lion shikar. His host was one of the first maharajas to merge his state with democratic India. Delicious fresh game was included in the picnic.

Inset. Interior of a shikar tent. These beautifully appointed tents were stocked with every conceivable luxury and worked as a perfect suite in the wilderness.

An older Maharaja Ganga Singh relaxes in a palki or a rough sedan chair, while on a lion shoot in the Gir Forest in 1940.

Inset. *The billiard room at Lallgarh Palace. Trophies from many hunts were displayed in rooms reserved exclusively for men. Here after dinner, over cigars and port, they could discuss an exciting hunt in the past while playing billiards on a hot Indian night.*

FESTIVALS AND WORSHIP

Some twenty miles outside the city of Bikaner stands a unique temple dedicated to Karniji, a woman who lived five centuries ago and was reputed to possess miraculous powers, such as the gift of prophecy. She is the guardian deity of the Bikaner dynasty because it was her predictions and blessings that guided Bika in the founding of his kingdom.

As a girl Karniji herded cattle and displayed great devotion to animals and birds, both wild and tame. In reverence to her memory, to this day any animal that strays into the temple is fed by her devotees. Karniji belonged to a local clan of troubadours, the Charans. According to legend, one of Karniji's clansmen placed the corpse of his only son before her and pleaded with the mystic lady to restore the child to life. Moved by the man's sorrow, Karniji entered into a deep trance in which she confronted Yama, the God of Death, and asked for the boy's soul. Yama did not yield to her appeal, answering that the child's soul had already been reincarnated in another body. An enraged Karniji vowed that none of her clansmen would ever come under Yama's power. She declared that when they died they would inhabit the bodies of rats, and when such rats died they would assume life as Charans once again.

Hundreds of rats scurry over the floors of Karniji's temple eating from huge bowls overflowing with sweetmeats, grain and milk donated by pilgrims. If an unwary visitor kills a rat, he has to donate a silver replica of his victim to the temple. And if a pilgrim sights a white rat he is believed to have been favoured by Karniji.

Other temples and shrines built by the pious abound in Bikaner. The best known amongst them is the Laxmi Narain temple where the maharaja is considered the main disciple. The city also contains the beautiful Bhandeshwar temple built by those professing the Jain faith. And everywhere outside the places of

Opposite. *The Lakshmi Narayanji Temple, dedicated to the Hindu God Vishnu and his consort, the Goddess Lakshmi. This was the most important shrine of the Bikaner dynasty, whose maharajas were considered its main disciples. In fact, the Bikaner State Anthem, a rousing tune sung in Rajasthani, illustrates the importance of the temple, as well as the reverence in which the people and rulers held the shrine of Karniji.*

Inset. *Maharaja Ganga Singh and guests driving past the Bhandeshwar Jain Temple in Bikaner. The 15th century Bhandeshwar temple is in the Muslim quarter of the old city of Bikaner, and stands on a high plinth with an Islamic style dome over its main entrance. The frescoes in the temple give a fascinating picture of Bikaner in the past.*

worship in this pious kingdom bards once recited ancient histories and sang the legends of religious mythology on holy days.

Holy days are celebrated in Bikaner's towns and villages with festivals, other functions and fairs, each having their individual form and rituals. They come with the change of seasons – Basant and Holi during the spring, Teej and Shivbari during the rains and Sharad Purnima and Diwali in autumn.

Many other individual festivals are also celebrated, especially Ganguar, the great folk festival of Rajasthan, when women give thanks for a happy married life, and young girls pray for a good husband. At this festival, idols of the God Shiva and his Consort Parvati are worshipped. At dawn maidens bathe idols of the God and Goddess and then decorate them with fresh blossoms, and at sunset place lit lamps in front of them. The Teej of Bhadwa is another important ceremony for the women of Bikaner. Wives fast for their husbands all day and then at night, having donned rich garments, they worship the moon with offerings of water.

The traditional fair of Shivbari remains a popular celebration. A few miles outside the city of Bikaner is a temple dedicated to Shiva, built on the banks of a large reservoir of rain water. In the month of Shrawan, when the moon is full, people come to worship the idol of Lord Shiva at this temple, with its battlements and dome shimmering in the moonlight.

The birthday of Lord Krishna is celebrated with nights of devotional music in the temples, and the festival of lights, Diwali, is celebrated throughout Bikaner with fireworks and lit lamps. Holi, the spring festival of colour, is celebrated with great abandon. The revellers spray each other with coloured water well into the night, unlike other places in India, where the festival ends decorously at noon.

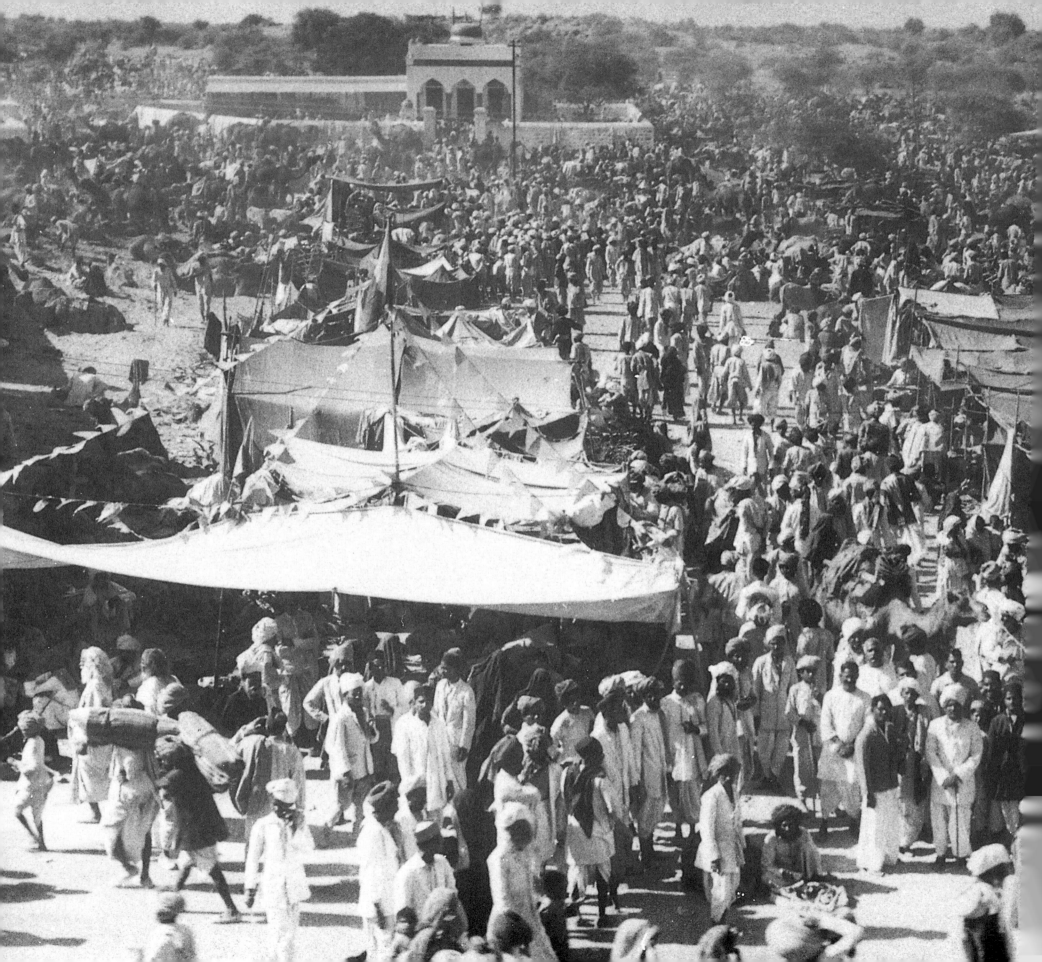

Opposite. A fair at Kolayat, 27 miles from Bikaner City. Villagers travelled many miles to attend these traditional holy-day fairs, where, in a festive atmosphere, cattle, grain and local handicrafts were traded. Kolayat is one of sixty-four sacred spots for Hindu pilgrims to visit. It was here during Vedic times that the great sage Kapil Muni spent a period in contemplation.

Above. Women performing the dandya ras or the stick dance, popular during many of Bikaner's festivals, particularly Holi, the Festival of Colour.

Below. Women holding butter lamps and auspicious tokens such as coconuts and banana leaves. The coconut is considered auspicious because it is a complete fruit — every part of it having a use.

The Hanuman Temple, Bikaner.
This temple is dedicated to the
monkey god, Hanuman, who
accompanied Lord Ram Chandraji
in his battle against Sri Lanka.

Opposite. The traditional
Rajasthan domes of a Hindu temple
at Rathangarh, some 25 miles from
Bikaner City.

VICEREGAL VISITS

In the reign of Maharaja Ganga Singh there was a constant stream of visitors to Bikaner, particularly in the winter months, known as "The Cold Season." The most formal of the Maharaja's guests were the Viceroys of India, rigid in demeanour when they paid state visits to Indian kingdoms as representatives of the King-Emperor, and more importantly, as the Paramount Power in India.

The moment a viceroy stepped off his white train to the thunder of a 31-gun salute, strict etiquette prevailed. Much time was wasted measuring the length of the red carpet on which the viceroy advanced to greet the ruler. Every item in the viceroy's programme was governed by ceremony. The visit, which usually lasted three days, was filled with functions: military reviews, the laying of foundation stones, a state banquet, and finally a grand durbar with the British viceroy seated to the right of the Indian ruler, underlining the proud power of Pax Britannica.

Ganga Singh put the hours between viceregal functions to good use, by convincing the visiting viceroy to endorse enlightened measures that were in progress in Bikaner and thus gaining approval for ambitious projects for the benefit of his people. Indeed, as the years passed, his model state became the envy of British administrators of the Indian Empire. The days of Ganga Singh's youth, when the Viceroy, Lord Elgin, wrote of him in his photo album as "a pleasant and interesting chief of sixteen", had long passed when another viceroy, Lord Linlithgow, raising a toast to the Maharaja on the occasion of his Golden Jubilee, said:

Opposite. Dancing girls perform after a banquet for the Viceroy, Lord Hardinge, at the Junagadh Fort in 1912.

Below. Maharaja Sadul Singh showing Lady Mountbatten an old Bikaner coin in 1949.

"The celebrations which are now taking place mark the Jubilee of the Ruler of one of the most conspicuous and progressive States in India; a Ruler, too, who has achieved for himself an outstanding position in India and the Empire. We are, all of us, familiar with the long record of distinguished service of Your Highness, in the field, as a Prince, as an administrator. To refer in detail to the many events of the long period of your rule is not possible in the short time at my disposal tonight."

A viceregal visit ended with the Viceroy taking formal leave of the Maharaja at the station before stepping smartly from the edge of the red carpet onto the steps of his white train. The Viceroy of India was the only personage in the subcontinent allowed to travel on a white train, another example of imperial superiority. Punishment for such arrogance was exacted by India's weather rather than by Indian rulers. One such phenomenon is illustrated in the diary of Yvonne Fitzroy, personal secretary to Lady Reading, wife of the Viceroy, when she had the misfortune to accompany the viceregal couple on a state visit during "The Hot Season": "We had heard much of the Viceregal train, even the Russian Imperial train could not compete with it for luxury, we were told, and were not disappointed. But all the luxury in the world cannot defeat this climate.... No screen was the least use against the dust – the fans merely circulated a hot, exhausted wind – door-handles nearly too hot to touch – beds far too hot to lie on – clothes, literally a painful necessity – and the hopeful rush to the cold-water tap greeted by a flow of nicely boiled water."

A group of British officers.

Opposite. The Viceroy, Lord Curzon, seated on Ganga Singh's right, during a visit to Bikaner in 1902. Curzon, who served as Viceroy from 1889 to 1904, upheld the privileges of Indian rulers but made sure that Britain's paramountcy was strengthened. While her husband governed the subcontinent, his American wife, Mary Curzon, seated on the Maharaja's left, kept an amusing journal of her travels in India.

Inset. *English burra sahibs and their mem sahibs seated in pairs on elephants. Bikaner. 1937.*

Above. *The Viceroy, Lord Curzon, and the Vicereine visiting Bikaner in 1902. They seem to be walking on an endless red carpet.*

Below. *The Vicereine, Lady Minto, wears a topee to protect her from the sun, while walking her pet dog on the platform of Bikaner Station in 1908.*

The Viceroy, Lord Irwin, and Lady Irwin bidding farewell to Maharaja Ganga Singh in 1927.

Inset. Members of the Viceroy's staff set off on a camel ride in 1912.

Inset. *The visit of Lord Linlithgow in 1937.*

Above. *Lord Willingdon arrives in Bikaner by plane. First by caravan, then by train and finally by aircraft came the Viceroys of India to the Kingdom of Bikaner. Ganga Singh, unlike many of his fellow maharajas, did not own an aircraft, as he did not enjoy flying.*

Below. *The visit of Lord Moutbatten to Maharaja Sadul Singh. 1949.*

The Viceroy, Lord Linlithgow, inaugurates the Golden Jubilee Museum in 1937.

Inset. The Linlithgows with Maharaja Ganga Singh in 1937 at Junagadh Fort, all elegantly attired in Western clothes. From the time the Maharaja ascended the throne, no Viceroy failed to pay a visit to Bikaner.

Maharaja Sadul Singh with Lord Mountbatten, the last Viceroy of British India and the first Governor-General of a free India. He visited Bikaner in 1949.

Opposite. *Lord Linlithgow inspecting the guard-of-honor at Lallgarh Palace.*

The wedding in 1930 of Prince
Kumar Bheem Sing of Kota and
Princess Shiv Kumari of Bikaner,
the daughter of Maharaja Ganga
Singh, was an event of great
extravagance. The Kingdom of
Kota in southern Rajasthan was
wealthy and active, its people were
devoted to various trades and its
fields made verdant by the wide
River Chambal that ran along its
borders. The old city-palace of Kota
conformed to the usual pattern of
such buildings, but at the beginning
of this century the ruler of Kota,
Maharao Umed Singh II, decided
to erect a new palace, the architect
of which was Sir Swinton Jacob
who had built the Lallgarh Palace
in Bikaner. In Kota, Sir Swinton
produced a sedately Anglicised
building with the addition of
Rajput decorative details. Thus
when the Princess Shiv Kumari of
Bikaner arrived at the palace as a
bride she found many similarities to
her own home. And this palace
remains the residence of the same
Prince and Princess Bheem Sing.

Opposite. Singers at the wedding.

Left. The bridegroom is followed by
Maharaja Ganga Singh and
Maharaja Jumar Sadul Singh, who
arranged the marriage of their
children in their infancy.

The wedding of Prince Karni Singh of Bikaner to the Princess Sushila Kumari of Durangpur in 1944. This hard, hilly land was dominated by the Bhils — fierce tribals whom the ancestors of Princess Sushila Kumari, the bride of Bikaner's Prince Karni Singh, subdued in the 13th century when they came to seek their fortune, leaving their ancestral home in Mewar, later known as Udaipur. The Princess had lived in Durangpur's 18th century palace built in granite and serpentine quarried within the state. This palace evolved into a honeycombed extravaganza of passages, balconies, pleasure pavilions and twisted pillars. On this page we see the Princess' dowry including precious silver thals, or serving dishes, priceless Oriental carpets and other essentials of a royal Indian household.

Opposite. The people of Bikaner bring wedding gifts to their Princess Sushila Kumari on the occasion of her marriage.

The wedding of Princess Sashil Kumari of Bikaner, the daughter of Maharaja Ganga Singh, to Maharaja Kumar Bhagwat Singh of Udaipur in 1940 was an occasion for particular rejoicing. The Udaipur – or Mewar – royal family (whose chief bore the title of Maharana) was considered the premier house of Rajputana due to their ancient lineage, reputed to go back to the sun itself. The city of Udaipur, to which the royal bridegroom belonged, was also famous for its tranquil lakes and creamy palaces. Another reason for the eminence of its reigning family was the aggressive resistance of their feudal ancestors to Muslim rule. The Maharanas of Udaipur never gave their daughters in marriage to the Moghul emperors, unlike other Rajput rulers, many of whose women entered the Imperial harem.

Above. The bridegroom's procession with the bride in a palki or covered palanquin. The bride's maid-servants went with her to her new home.

Below. A band marches past Bikaner Fort.

Opposite. Maharaja Ganga Singh and Maharana Bhopal Singh of Udaipur in the Bikaner state carriage. A cripple, the Maharana was for much of his life largely confined to his palace.

Overleaf. A procession of the bridegroom at night.

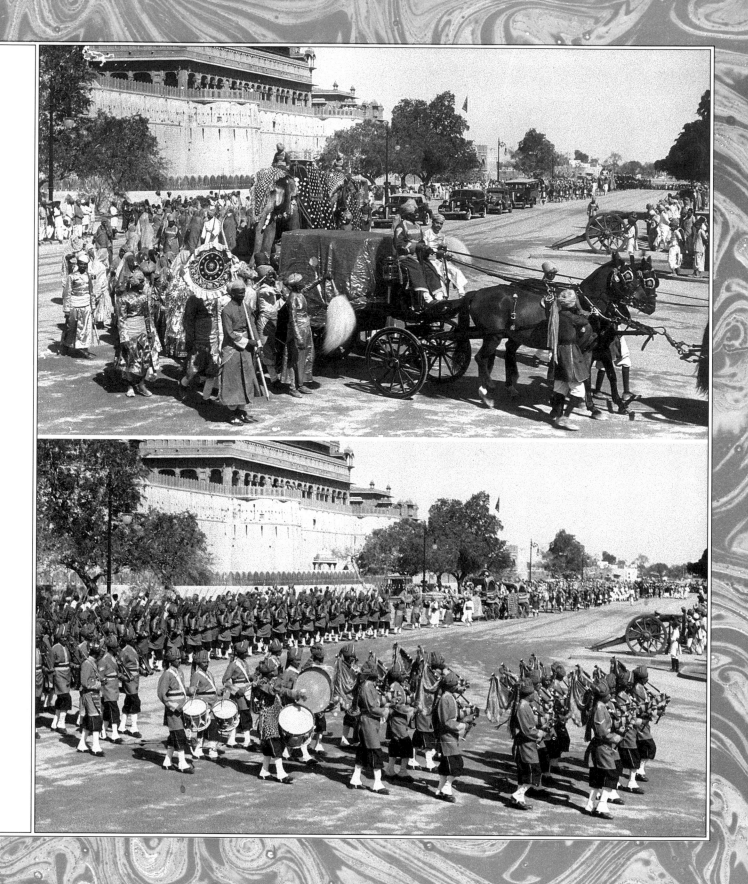

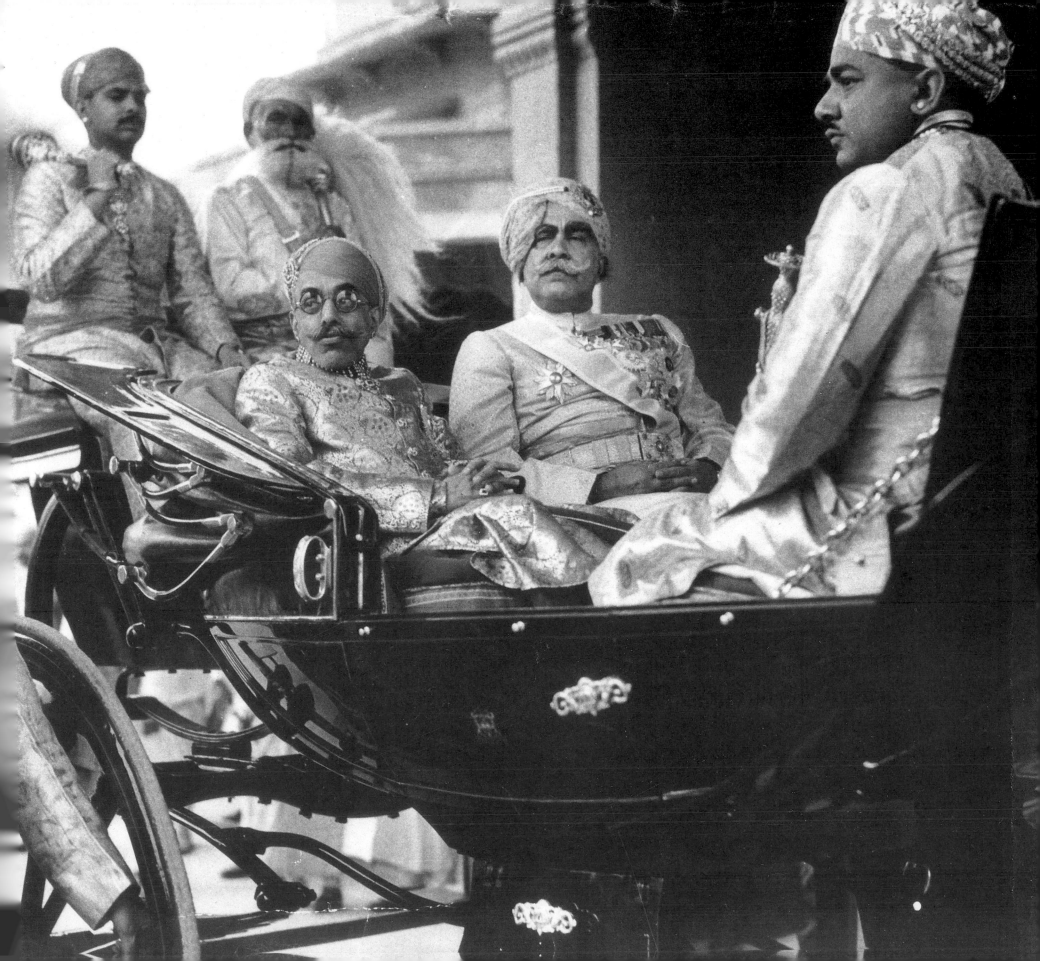

Because the House of Udaipur was acknowledged as the defender of Rajput purity, Rajputana's kings sought the prestige of matrimonial matches with members of that family. In the early 19th century the powerful Maharajas of Jaipur and Jodhpur were even prepared to go to war to win the hand of Udaipur's Princess Krishna Kumari. To prevent such a disaster, the beautiful girl sacrificed herself by taking poison. This tragic incident led one callous British official to remark: ''Women should die young and by violent means if they desire the reputation of their beauty to live for posterity.''

As soldiers demonstrated the power of an Indian king, female dancers and singers displayed the splendour of his court. Under the patronage of the Maharaja, they performed on holy days, weddings, birthdays and other happy occasions, and their presence was considered propitious at such functions. These girls sang the praises of the ruler's lineage, and their Bardic ballads served as a link between the court and the people.

Opposite. *Singers between performances.*

Above. *A singer entertains royal guests at Lallgarh Palace.*

Below. *Dancing girls rest before performing for their royal audience.*

A RAJPUT AT WAR

Fierce warriors, proud of their martial traditions, the Rajputs of Bikaner engaged in more than sixty campaigns in the period preceding the advent of the British Raj. Bika's battles to establish his kingdom were followed by the wars waged by his descendants in the service of the Moghul emperors in such distant territories as Afghanistan, Baluchistan, Sind, the Deccan, and Bengal. Circumstances altered with the coming of the British. Nevertheless, the opportunity to give battle presented itself during the Great Uprising of 1857, when Maharaja Sardar Singh led his warriors to the aid of the beleaguered British.

Inspired by his military heritage, Maharaja Ganga Singh had from boyhood been a keen soldier. After receiving his military training, first with his own forces at home, and subsequently with a crack regiment of the Indian Army at Deoli, he was gazetted in 1900 an honorary major of the British Army – the youngest major at his time. Promotions came in quick succession: Lt. Colonel in 1909, Colonel in 1910, Major General in 1917, Lt. General in 1930, and finally full General in 1937.

The Maharaja was the first Indian ruler to cross the sea to wage war for the British Empire. At the head of the Ganga Risala Camel Corps he sailed to China in 1901 to join the British forces in crushing the Boxer Rebellion. Raised by the young Maharaja, this camel corps was well equipped and run on modern lines with a strength of 500 men. The regiment was named the "Ganga Risala" after its ruler and acquitted itself courageously on its arrival in Tienstin, earning mention in despatches. Two years later, when the

Opposite. *Maharaja Ganga Singh with members of the Ganga Risala Camel Corps, which was an efficient unit for desert warfare trained in the most modern methods of battle. Their camels were perfectly behaved, although on rare occasion the odd animal could prove stubborn, particularly when being put on ship to go to war. Sometimes obstinate, camels were wrapped in great nets and hauled aboard.*

Inset. *Every year a contingent of the Camel Corps participates in the Republic Day Parade with their caparisoned camels and splendidly uniformed and turbaned riders. And when the contingent comes down the wide avenue that divides the central vista of India's capital, they are greeted by the parade's huge audience with much applause.*

theatre of war moved to Somaliland, Ganga Singh was represented by the Bikaner troops, though he did not take the field personally.

At the outbreak of the Great War, the Maharaja placed himself and his soldiers once again at the service of the British Empire. On August 25, 1914, Ganga Singh exhorted his troops: "Remember, my brave men, what our traditions are. We came to Bikaner as fighting men. Soldiers we are; and soldiers we have ever since remained. We fought in China and in Somaliland. Now we go to fight again; may God and Sri Karniji, our protectress, bless and preserve you. May you render meritorious services... and return home safe and victorious!"

Ganga Singh then proceeded to Flanders, where he was appointed to the staff of Field Marshal Sir John French, the Commander-in-Chief of the British Force, while his camel corps served in Egypt against the Turks and also helped in patrolling the Suez Canal. In 1915, the Maharaja took part in fierce desert fighting with his troops. Sir James Willcocks, who commanded the Indian forces, wrote to Ganga Singh after the war: "I always recall your good work during those terrible days! Never afraid of mud or discomfort or anything else, you showed a fine spirit, Maharaja, worthy of your great name and race."

By the time that World War II broke out, Ganga Singh held the rank of full General in the British Army. In October 1941, ignoring all suggestions that he was too old for the battlefield, he engaged in active service in the Middle East, a mere two years before his death.

Inset. *Representation of the Bikaner State Armies.*

Above. *The Bikaner troops being addressed at Junagadh Fort on August 6, 1914 by Maharaja Ganga Singh prior to their departure for the Middle Eastern front during World War I. Maharaja Ganga Singh, after being posted at the Flanders Front, served at the head of the Ganga Risala Camel Corps at Ismalia when the Turkish Army was approaching the Suez Canal in February 1915. In the ensuing encounter the Maharaja and his unit took part in the action, with Ganga Singh using his rifle to great effect. And when the Turks retreated from the Canal, the Ganga Risala pursued the enemy.*

Below. *Four officers – the ones in dark uniforms belonged to the Dungar Lancers, and the ones in white uniforms to the Ganga Risala Camel Corps.*

Opposite. *Maharaja Ganga Singh and the Ganga Risala Camel Corps departing in 1901 for China to fight in the Boxer Rebellion.*

Opposite. *It is extremely difficult for a camel to jump, its legs being so thin that a fall could cripple the beast permanently. Notwithstanding, the officers of the Camel Corps trained their mounts to jump as perfectly as horses in a steeplechase.*

Above. *The Ganga Risala Camel Corps in the Thar Desert. This corps, founded by Maharaja Ganga Singh as a young man, saw action in the China War of 1900, the Somaliland Campaign in Africa from 1902 to 1904, in World War I and World War II in the Middle East, and in Sind, where it helped suppress the Hurs in 1941. In 1951, after Independence, the Ganga Risala Camel Corps and another camel battalion, the Jaisalmer Risala, were merged and given the name of Ganga-Jaisalmer Risala. In 1954 this Camel Corps joined the forces of the Grenadier Regiment of the Indian Army and became the 13 Grenadiers.*
Above. *The Ganga Risala Camel Corps in the desert.*

Below. *The corps with small cannon trooping past the Viceroy, Lord Irwin, in 1927. The manner in which the soldiers and camels handled the guns is recorded in the Golden Jubilee Book: "A special feature of the performance was a musical ride by the Camel Pack Battery. This Force, which is unique in the world, consists of four modern 2.75" guns, each of which when dismounted is carried by four camels. The guns can be mounted or dismounted in less than two minutes. For the musical ride, each gun was drawn by two pairs of camels, performing the most difficult evolutions racing at a fast trot without so much as falling out of step and frequently cutting into each other's path with only a foot or two to spare."*

THE GOLDEN JUBILEE

In 1937 Maharaja Ganga Singh completed fifty years of his reign. When his subjects requested permission to celebrate the occasion, the Maharaja deferred his consent. The monsoon rains, never partial to his domain, were unduly late and Ganga Singh was adamant that there could be no jubilee festivities when drought threatened Bikaner. Weeks passed and the scorching sky showed no hint of clouds. People stopped thinking of celebration and began instead to prepare for famine. In desperation, Ganga Singh travelled to the village of Deshnoke to pray for assistance from the kingdom's guardian deity, Karniji. For days he stayed in the temple praying for rain. In the middle of September, when the monsoon season was over and there remained no hope of rain, above the heads of the villagers crowded outside the temple there appeared a single cloud in the sky. The villagers rushed into the temple to call the ruler to come out and see the rain clouds massing on the horizon. As rain drenched the parched land, the Maharaja at last gave his consent to celebrate his Golden Jubilee.

The ceremonies and rituals with which Ganga Singh's subjects celebrated their ruler's fifty years of enlightened government lasted an entire year.

One of them is described in the Golden Jubilee Book – the occasion being a public address at the Junagadh Fort on October 30, 1937.

Opposite. Maharaja Ganga Singh in 1937 holding durbar in the Vikram Bilas Throne Room at Junagadh Fort. On his birthday, during the Golden Jubilee year, the Maharaja received a long line of persons who did obeisance to their ruler. First came the princes followed by chieftains, ministers, officers and officials and, at the very end, the palace servants and artisans. Each man bowed three times before the ruler and made an offering of a gold coin as a token of tribute.

Above. Maharaja Ganga Singh wearing a cape with the Order of the Knight Commander of the Star of India. By the time of the Golden Jubilee Ganga Singh's full titles read: General His Highness Maharajadhiraj Raj Rajeshwar Narendra Shiromani Maharajah Sri Ganga Singhji Bahadur, G.C.S.I., G.C.I.E., G.C.V.O., G.B.E., K.C.B., LL.D., Maharaja of Bikaner.

"Escorted by his bodyguard the Maharaja drove slowly past the cheering crowd and through the spiked gates of the fort, which are adorned with the marks of many little hands – hands of consorts, in days long past, who had touched them all before following their lords to the funeral pyre. Outwardly, the scene of the ritual that followed was as it had been from the time when those little hands were tremulously raised. The brilliant coloured durbar dress, the jewels and swords, the greetings and all the ceremonial belonged to the Rajput splendour of bygone centuries. The glories of the past came to light and the picture seemed to be a reflection of the brillant court scenes of the past that are depicted on the priceless old paintings adorning the galleries of the fort. It was medieval Rajputana that faced the spectator in the large hall with its richly carved walls and ceilings. But when the ritual was over and the Maharaja rose to address the audience, the modern ruler came to the forefront. In reviewing the principal events of his rule he laid stress on his people. To the people he accordingly gave back, in the shape of beneficent institutions, the donations which they had generously contributed to the Golden Jubilee Fund, and in pointing out that he had ever endeavoured to bring to Bikaner the advantages of modern progress, he announced the introduction of numerous reforms which constituted another step forward in the modernisation of the state."

Maharaja Ganga Singh's procession was described in the Golden Jubilee Book. "It was from the courtyard of this Fort that the procession set out to the Temple of Sri Lakshmi Narayanji. The leading elephant carried the State Flag. It was followed by units of the Bikaner Army, including two batteries of the Camel Pack Artillery, and a detachment of the Bikaner Camel Corps, the Mounted Lancers and the Infantry, all in their magnificent full dress uniforms. Other elephants followed with the State regalia; and after the thirteen musical instruments, the silver palanquins, bullock chariots and lead horses had passed, the Maharaja's own party followed on more elephants. First came the Heir-Apparent on a great tusker, surrounded by other Members of the Reigning Family on horseback. Next rode His Highness on a magnificent ten-foot elephant, gorgeously caparisoned in cloths of blue velvet and silver and a variety of jewels and ornaments. The Maharaja himself, seated in the golden howdah, wore a white Durbar coat, a saffron-coloured turban, all his orders, decorations and war medals. He was attended by some of the principal feudal Chiefs of the State. The Maharaja's bodyguard and the Dungar Lancers wound up the procession."

Above. A battery of caparisoned elephants await the Maharaja outside the Junagadh Fort.

Below. The Maharaja climbs the steps of the Lakshmi Narayanji Temple for the thanksgiving ceremony.

Opposite. He rides in majesty on a 10-foot high pachyderm.

During his reign Ganga Singh gave generous amounts of money to all religions in his state – Hindu, Muslim, Sikh, Jain and Christian. And all his subjects, rich or poor, gave donations for the Golden Jubilee Fund knowing it would be spent on charity. Here, the people of the city observe the Maharaja's progress from Junagadh Fort to the Laxmi Narayanji Temple. The following passage from the Golden Jubilee Book records the atmosphere at that moment: "The people raised their folded hands in the greeting and shouted Khama – the local equivalent of hurrah. Roses and other flowers – great rarities in dry Bikaner – were showered on the Maharaja and his son from the housetops while women sang songs of rejoicing. This was the first of a remarkable series of popular demonstrations.''

According to custom, in a "Tuladan" ceremony the maharaja was weighed against gold. The weighing took place on a pair of large scales set up in the "Yagya Shala", a beautiful sandstone pavilion which stands in the grounds of Lallgarh Palace. While priests chanted sacred Hindu hymns, Ganga Singh took his seat on one of the scales. The other was loaded with ingots of pure gold from the state's treasury. Gold to the value of Rs.3,021,915 was balanced against the Maharaja's weight of 14 stones and 8 pounds. Then, the cash equivalent of the gold and other sums of money were donated to the Golden Jubilee Fund, and used for charity within the state.

Above. Prince Sadul Singh with his two sons, Karni Singh and Amar Singh, during the Golden Jubilee.

Below. Maharaja Ganga Singh salutes in his Rolls while the state anthem is played. Rolls-Royce found their biggest customers among the maharajas, who had the cars adapted for every use and occasion. This elegant cabriolet model was perfect for parades.

ACKNOWLEDGEMENTS

This book was made possible by so many people that I find it difficult adequately to express my appreciation.

Foremost, in Bikaner, my special thanks go to Princess Rajyashree Kumari. Also to Sri Dalip Singh and Sri Hanuwant Singh and the other members of the Maharaja Ganga Singhji Trust for their help and generosity in making available to me archival and photographic material for the book.

In New Delhi, for their erudition and advice, I am grateful to Martand Singh, Princess Hershad Kumari, Mahijit Singh Jhala, Raj Srivastava and especially to my sister, Gita Mehta. In the pictorial aspects of the book, my gratitude to Aditya Patankar, Harminder Kumar and Ravi Pasricha.

Finally, in London, I am indebted to David Cholomondeley and Nicholas Ward Jackson for making available fascinating material on the Bikaner of the past.

NAVEEN PATNAIK

BIBLIOGRAPHY

ALLEN, Charles. *Lives of the Indian Princes*. London, 1984.

BENCE-JONES, Mark. *The Viceroys of India*. London, 1982.

Bikaner Golden Jubilee Book, 1887-1937. Commemorative Volume. Bombay, 1937.

BROWN, P. *Indian Painting under the Mughals*. Oxford, 1924.

DEVRA, G.S.L., ed. *Maharaja Ganga Singhji; Centenary Volume*. Bikaner, 1980.

FITZROY, Yvonne. *Courts and Camps of India*. London, 1926.

GASCOIGNE, Bamber. *The Great Moghals*. London, 1971.

IVORY, James, *Autobiography of a Princess*. New York, 1975.

LORD, John. *The Majarajas*. London, 1971.

PANIKKAR, K.M. *1His Highness The Maharaja of Bikaner*. London, 1937.

SARKAR, J. *History of Aurangzeb*. Calcutta, 1925.

SINGH, Karni. *From Rome to Moscow: The Memoirs of an Olympic Trap Shooter*. New Delhi, 1982.

SINGH, Karni. *The Relations of the House of Bikaner with the Central Powers*. New Delhi, 1974.

SINGH, Kishore. *Bikaner: A Fifth Centenary Commemorative Volume*. New Delhi, 1989.

SINGH, Martand. *The Master Weavers*. Delhi, 1982.

SINGH, Raghubir. *Rajasthan*. New York, 1981.

SINGH, Y.P., ed. *Son of the Soil: Maharaja Ganga Singhji*. Bikaner, 1981.

SUNDARAM, V.A. *Benares Hindu University 1905-1935*. Foreword by H.H. The Maharajah of Bikaner. Varanasi, 1936.

THOMAS, P. *Festivals and Holidays of India*. Bombay, 1971.

TOD, James. *The Annals and Antiquities of Rajasthan*. Ed. by W. Crooke. London, 1920.

WORSWICK, Clark. *Princely India's Photographs by Raja Deen Dayal*. New York, 1980.